KV-702-992

THE SPACE BETWEEN

THE SPACE BETWEEN

Kate Dempsey

Doire Press

First published in March 2016

Doire Press
Aille, Inverin
Co. Galway
www.doirepress.com

Layout & cover design: Lisa Frank
Cover image: Kate Dempsey
Author photo: Pat Gorman

Printed by Clódóirí CL
Casla, Co. na Gaillimhe

Copyright © Kate Dempsey

ISBN 978-1-907682-41-4

All rights reserved. No part of this publication may be reproduced or transmitted in any form or by any means. This book is sold subject to the usual trade conditions.

We gratefully acknowledge the assistance of Kildare County Council Arts Service.

CONTENTS

It's What You Put into It   11

While It Lasted   12

The Belt   14

Reaching Agreement   15

David is Dancing   16

The Full Experience   18

Drunk the Poet   19

Drinking Now   20

I Could Lie   21

Amsterdam Otto Recommends   22

Let's Go Driving   23

Southern Roads   24

Two Almond Granitas in Soller   26

The Light Fantastic   28

We are off the Map   29

They Enter the Dojo by Separate Ways   30

Prunes   31

Snow Women   32

Running Out   33

Elsewhere in the Now   34

Regeneration   35

The Flight of Swallows   36

Life Under the Lens   38

She is Mercury   39

Thorium 238   40

Sulfur   41

Hydrogen   42

Equations on Waking   43

Lump   44

She Stoops to Conker   45

Conker   46

Monaghan Mosquitoes   47

That Broken Pot   48

Unintentional Installation   49

Grange Castle Haiku   50

Karl   52

Flaming for Vincent   56

Lying in our Morning Bed   58

Slow Poison 1944   59

Hubie is Wearing his Uniform   60

We Keep our Old Defences   62

Verbatim   63

An Agreeable Afternoon   64

She was the Queen of the Butterfly Bun   65

Email, Three Poems Attached   66

By Strawberry Beds   68

Essence   70

Pure Class   71

Only Six Minutes of Normal Time Remain   72

A City with Stones of Gold   74

Tell Me about your Scar   75

What to do with my Ashes   76

Mash   77

Acknowledgements   78

About the Author   79

Dedicated with much love to my parents, John and Avis Prior, who always believed in me. Or if sometimes they had doubts, never let me know.

It's What You Put Into It

For Grace

On the last day of term
you brought home a present,
placed it under the tree,
a light, chest-shaped mystery
wrapped in potato stamped paper
intricate with angels and stars.

Christmas morning
you watched as we opened it,
cautious not to tear the covering.
Inside, a margarine tub, empty.
Do you like it? eyes huge.
It's beautiful.
What is it, sweetheart?
A box full of love, you said.

You should know, O my darling girl,
it sits on the dresser still
and from time to time, we open it.

While It Lasted

One day when I was thirteen, my mother's hands fell off.
They rolled under the table, giving the cat a bit of a turn.
We looked at them but they gave no sign,
a couple of twitches and that was that.
Mum stood at the chopping board as still as a goalpost.

Dad made her lie on the chaise while he put on the potatoes.
She lay holding her bloody stumps high
so they wouldn't make a mess of the gold velvet.
Dad cooked the dinner and dished up.
We gave her a plate too but how could she eat it?
'Don't mind me,' she said.
I gave her a bite of my ham and all of my broccoli.

Dad asked if he should call the doctor.
'I don't want to make a fuss.'
The cat jumped on her lap but, having no hands,
Mum couldn't stroke her nor tip her off.
She rubbed her head against my mother's cheek
then left to wind in and out of my legs instead
purring, which she never did before.

'You go off and enjoy yourself,' Mum said
so I went and watched *Top of the Pops*
with the door shut, tied up my school blouse,
danced on the rug like Pan's People
and didn't turn down the volume for the loud ones.
Dad asked if she wanted to go to the pub.
'I don't want to be in the way,' she said
and read the same page of the paper over and over.

The next day I made my own school lunch
and had toast for breakfast instead of Weetabix.
Dad put Mum's hands neatly in a Tupperware box
and stored them next to the lentils.
'Don't worry about me,' said Mum. 'I'll get by.'

Weeds grew, dust gathered and the cat shed ginger hairs.
We lived on fish and chips and Chinese.
Dad shopped and washed, I cooked and cleaned.
We gave up ironing and cabbage and mowing the lawn.
Mum's stumps healed up nicely.
On the shelf next to the mouldy lentils,
her hands shrivelled like marigold seeds.

Then the cat caught a blackbird, ate it
and sicked it up all over the hall floor.
We stared at the lake of vomit and feathers.
'It was good while it lasted,' Mum sighed.
She opened the Tupperware with her teeth,
screwed both hands back in
and filled the bucket with hot soapy water.

The Belt

When the school roof shook with the chatter
or someone laughed when Jimmy did that jerky thing
when Kirsteen gave cheek again or Greg showed his glass eye
when Fiona made orange squash run down her nose
or Drew blotted ink on Aileen's good jersey
when someone scratched a bad word on a chair
and no one told, though we all knew it was David
when a corner brawl broke out
or everyone fought over Greens beat Blues

if you threw snowballs at Teacher's bike
if you wrote on the blackboard at break
if you looked out of the window
if you were late
if you chewed your hair
if you spoiled your jotter
if you forgot your homework
if you mixed up your letters
if you sang out of tune

that's when Teacher opened her fliptop desk with a meaningful look
and the sleeping black mamba uncurled and reared up its full length,
we, sick and silent, squirmed on our hands
watched its thick body thrash, its buckle eye squint.

It was a fistful of wasps in your crossed hands.
It was red as the sunset and ten million degrees.
She would look at your face and her eyes would go narrow.
If you didn't cry, she was disappointed.

Reaching Agreement

And I realise I'm listening to your voice,
not your speech, nor any of your points,
though you've considered every one,
deliberated for hours, weighed the arguments.
But I'm zoned out to the latent rumble
that's near the limits of perception,
tuned to a harmonic that sets whales singing.
The enveloping timbre would sway a jury,
would sell a pianola.

Your lips move but I'm hearing
the way you taste the space between your words,
phrasing so there's something more than silence,
an emphasis pregnant with promise.
I'm wondering how it would sound
if you were murmuring my name,
intoning, moaning the buttered safety of it.

Your breath is measured, the rhythms soothe me,
cajole and warm me
to an undeniable, joyous
'Yes,'
to whatever it was you said.

David is Dancing

David has a long braid
It whips around his body
in elliptical orbit

After dinner he dances barefoot
His slim hands stroke the air
his body throws river shadows

Piano chords swim around him
flit, swirl, explore dark corners
like lush, jungle fish

The music room whirls counterpoint
Outside the garden turns in time
Weeds throw up their lovely heads and howl

The sycamores creak and stretch
dip branches in the lake
to splash up a rhythm

And the drumlins from Newbliss to Cootehill
shrug off their megaliths
and nudge each other closer

The dark lake reflects
the night sky
as the lake always does

The stars dance too
the nebulas with their distant thrumming
light up David's face

And we drink him in
record and itemise him
with sounds, shapes, words

but captivated as one
in this stolen time,
precious as moonwater

Together on this evening,
in this moment that flickers and,
with a swish of David's fingers, fades.

The Full Experience

As the lights dim, he ambles by,
fumbles in his pocket,
muscles shape his thin shirt,
spicy aftershave,
hair velvet-shorn,
long lean legs, soft leather belt,
and the grace of Fred Astaire.

In another life,
in an other life
I follow him to the foyer.
We scoop five flavours of Ben and Jerry's
and climb to the projection room.
As the film reels overhead,
we rip off our clothes and make love,
dirty sticky love,
down among the popcorn.

In a life,
in this life
I note him passing,
reach over and squeeze your thigh.
You take my hand,
the music builds, we face the screen.
I prefer the front row for the full experience.

Drunk the Poet

Stewed features lean in, eyes checking
that I'm still listening
and I am still listening.
He's dragging me down a path to God-knows-where.
'Are you with me?' I am,
poised to catch him when he falls
for fall he will, he has no doubt about it.

He embarks on a rant against rhymes, form,
tearing into line endings and the nausea when it's
wrong, throws up the vowel sounds, juxtapositions
and stanzas fully formed.
He launches a tirade on readings where no one came
or he stole the show from the headline act
and how the kids think he's great.

And I think he's great,
a great waste of talent spilling from the glass
and I want to save him, I do.
He needs someone to mind him,
listen to and forgive him —
God forbid — sleep with him.
But that's a good deal to ask, I can see
a lot of worry, stains and troubles ahead,
lost days, late nights, all this
for the sake of a few poems?

What if, after all this, he wasn't, won't be —
what if he's not that great?

Drinking Now

This wine wants to have its way with you.
It wants to seduce you with spicy notes,
dreams of long, lazy dinners and long lost loves,
warm you, make you smile, lower your defences.
This wine wants to come at you from a different angle,
touch you in unfamiliar places,
your tongue, your mouth, yes, your lips.
See swirling within, the silky undercurrents —
they have something to say.

This wine wants to uncork you,
tickle your taste buds, your fancy, your fantasy.
Sniff it, sip it, gulp and pour it,
there purely for the revel,
the reveal of imaginative insinuations —
crickets on a summer night,
the empty beach at darkfall,
salty waves and salty wives,
the extravagant promises of emotional men.

Now sliding down behind your breast bone,
this wine brings a tingle to your fingers,
a softness to your gaze,
cherry tinges to your cheeks.
This wine wants to get fresh, to question your reserve.
It blurs the boundaries,
loosens your larynx, maybe later you'll sing again,
dance to praise the winemakers,
all hail the oenologists.
Honour the care taken in the making,
sun warmed, barrel aged.
The long finish lingers
like a memory,
like a kiss.

I Could Lie

I could make it up.
I could tell you it was in a fancy restaurant
cushioned in raspberry mousse sweeter than velvet.
I could say it was a summer night
a plump moon
pink champagne, roses.
I could lie and say it took me by surprise
I cried
he cried
diners clapped, waiters cheered
fireworks filled the sky
harps, violins.

But it was not so.

It was a Saturday morning
a supermarket run
an underground car park.
It was a zip stuck on my jacket.
He knelt down
jeans skimming an oil stain.
I looked at his head,
touched the thinning patch,
he so tall, no one knew it was there
but me.

His hands tugging the zip,
his breath steaming like exhaust fumes
and I said 'While you're down there.
While you're down there,
why don't you ask me?'
and smiling up, he did.

I could tell you
it was like this.

Amsterdam Otto Recommends

And an emerald, square cut, says Otto,
green for Ireland or something like that, offset just so.

Diamonds on black felt sparkle under
halogen lamps like a night sky in the polders.

We nod, dazed as the guilders churn
to madness. He tweezers the tiny stone, turns

so it glitters like Elizabeth Taylor's first;
one month's salary in one small burst.

Of course, in a few years, he says, glancing up,
but not at me, you can trade up.

Let's Go Driving

Let's go driving nowhere, love.
The skies are bursting,
the moon is young.
Turn up the heat, demist the glass,
flick the wipers double-time
to catch your pulse and mine.
Let's leave behind the orange glow
clear the front until
all we can see ahead
is stars.

Southern Roads

We are a small bit lost.
The map seems precise,
along a forested road,
past a tumbledown house,
left here, right, straight on.
Travelling down a lane
which becomes a byway.
On the narrow track
clover and milk thistle grow —
a meridian of petals.
We plough on together,
it's too late to turn around,
green staining our wheels,
across a wide meadow
with the slightest of ruts
leading over the rise.
A route existed here
once.

Once
a route existed here,
leading over the rise
with the slightest of ruts,
across a wide meadow.
Green staining our wheels,
it's too late to turn around,
we plough on together.
A meridian of petals —
clover and milk thistle grow
on the narrow track
which becomes a byway.
Travelling down a lane,
left here, right, straight on,
past a tumbledown house,
along a forested road.
The map seems precise.
We are a small bit lost.

Two Almond Granitas in Soller
For Denis

In the middle sea of love is an island
beach-fringed, lush and stony within.

On the island of love a wooden train
clatters by pines and orange groves

rattles affably through mountains
to the terminus in the town

where solid buildings lean in
and whisper tales of love.

In the town of love is a striking church
one side of a sun-drenched plaza

diagonaled by the port tram
which dings through parting crowds

and shadows of Miró and Picasso
sip cafés con leche at a pavement café.

In the midst of the plaza of love
sits a singer, hat and leather waistcoat

guitar clutched like a golden lover
strings stroked like a plaintive suitor

reaching, keening the high notes
and singing a song of love.

Sweetening the singer of love
are percussions of cups and coffee spoons

camera clicks and phone trills
the gentle murmur of café talk.

In the shade of the corner rest
two lovers with two almond granitas

condensation slipping, dripping
down the glass like sweat on skin

pooling to the silvered table top
where your hand holds mine.

The Light Fantastic

Beyond the back of beyond
along a high-hedged meander,
a heavy pause rested
like the silence on an empty beach
after a surfers' wave.
I sat with my finger on the map
as you tried to read between the folds.

You pulled over at a sign saying
Dancer Cows Crossing
and we watched the Friesian hoofers
pirouette out of the field,
conga up the lane
and soft-shoe-shuffle into the yard.

The farmer quickstepped the gate shut,
and we tripped on.

We are off the Map

We are off the map, searching for street signs.
Market Square: a couple in the corner
are rutting under an orange lamp, not twenty yards off,
his jeans dropped, belt dangling,
her skirt hitched, legs bare around him, back to the red brick,
rain splatting, music spilling from the pub.
We jolt, withdraw wordless.

The Shambles: Only after, do we pause to think,
was it passion or was she pushing him away,
slammed against that wall?
Were his hands supporting or restraining,
she moaning or crying?
We too shook, too absorbed in our own reactions
to check directions.

They Enter the Dojo by Separate Ways
For Rose

Her thoughts are the river
the river rushes on
her fears are a torrent
her him them then
the steady stones
are water worn
the lush bank —
oxlips and wild garlic
her feet are bare
the water cool
she can watch from there
here now soon gone
she has her girls with her
she has their girls
her thoughts are the river
her fears feed the salty sea.

Prunes

I do not belong in this family, just so you know.
My real name is Princess Daffodil.
I don't know how I got here,
fairies maybe, a mix-up at the hospital.

My real Mummy and Daddy are King and Queen
and they love me very much and never argue
and one day they'll come in their golden coach
and take me away.

They won't shout or make me eat prunes;
they'll let me stay up late and watch TV whenever I want.
Just so you know, I'll be glad that day
and you'll be really, really sorry.

Snow Women

Do you remember that snow woman
on the slopes of Carrantuohill
that winter trek with Dad and Joe?
You and I turned back and they hiked on
across the brook on tipping stones.

We rolled her body, then her head,
shaped ample curves, fixed scrub for hair,
pebbled eyes, a twiggy pout,
you arched her brows and found
a branch to show the way.

She'll be spring melt, that I know,
gone to ground in a slow curtsey
but you and I remain bewintered;
the wrench of summer in between
too late to thaw.

Running Out

I mean to say
'Why is it so difficult?'
Doesn't he see it?
The empty roll.
The replacement standing fatly.
I mean to say
'Just spring it out and change it.
Is it so hard?'
My grandmother told me
'Men don't see dirt.'
Men don't see.
I mean to say
'Just change it, why can't you?'
I say
'Just change.'

Elsewhere in the Now

I should like to light out
pull on my purple hat and not come back
a foot passenger on a ferry,
by bike, by trundled train,
hitch-hiking at on-ramps
with a sign saying 'Anywhere but here'

I would grow my hair and dye it pink
linger somewhere hot
where a T-shirt will suffice from dawn to night
and stars splatter the sky
where siestas are acceptable
and slowly is the way

I would bake bread in a wood-fired oven,
grow onions and raspberries,
keep bees to listen to my stories
spread them across clover fields.
I'd have no papers, no number,
no yesterday, no tomorrow, no regrets.

Regeneration

The reason why
there's so much dust in this hoover bag
is that we renew each cell in our bodies
every seven years —
skin and bone, fat and muscle,
heart and mind, you name it, is shed.

Everything about you from when I first knew you
is replaced.
So when I say
you're not the man I thought you were,
you're not.
And I am not the girl you married either.

But what I can't figure is
if my brain is in this restoration,
why can I still remember
everything you said
everything I did
the night we met?

We drop our body crumbs together.
They gather under the furniture
finger with lip
knuckle with rib
and I suck them up
with the hoover.

The Flight of Swallows

A single swallow flies somehow
in the window, the gap she comes through

as thick as your hospital chart,
realises her mistake and skirts

the stitched screen, wheels, her wing an inch
from the ceiling and speeds once, twice

slap bang into the pane. I, standing
one boot on, one off, fluttering

as useless as when they restrained
you to deliver insulin,

the thin needles made you cry;
you held my wrist fast, as tight

as when your fist first grasped my hand.
She thumps into the glass again;

a clump of grey breast-down floats
to the floor. And she's flown so far

from that baked Sahara fringe,
to this cold north; all so pointless — breaking

on my frayed-sash window. And me,
my mouth again a soundless O.

I flap forward with one bare foot
to force the window perhaps or scoot

her out — there must be something I could
do. If I could take your place, I would.

She swoops around with one last sweep
of her tail, skims the ledge and escapes.

Life Under the Lens

Sue is at home in the lab. Microscopes
reduce problems to tiny parts; she copes,
concentrates on slides, focuses the lens,
avoids thoughts about her daughter, just hopes
she's at school and not skiving with her friends.

Her cancer research uses just the male
fruitflies. She's dissected three hundred in all
knocks them out first with carbon dioxide.
Analysing the numbers, she's hopeful,
though it's early days and the study's wide.

She has learnt to tell the sexes apart.
Her supervisor trained her in the art
of manipulating the forceps,
admires the skill with which she slows her heart,
steadies her hand, holds her breath and snips.

The flies have hatched within the day, still fresh,
they don't stay young for long, she takes ones less
toddlers, more youths; she's found that she enjoys
ripping the balls off these
adolescent boys.

She is Mercury

The elusive quicksilver
she runs rings around emperors,
breaks promises:
she says she'll be there around nine
all smoothness and glimmer
shimmering in her unique way
by eleven you're hot and flustered
calling her mobile
calling the hospitals —
this time she's really gone and done it.

Thorium 238

I am Thorium
luke on mi magnifisens an kwiver.
Yes, I can save de world,
D-fur de inevitabble 4 a millenium
wile u punie weeklings kerb
yr pathetic adickshun 2 fossle fules.

I will skwat on a shelf an woch
yr cowerin scientists run
Xperiment after Xperiment —
presher, timing, tempretcher —
crunch de numbers lyk fish bowens.
Den yr blinkerd engineres fiddl an swet
2 get it 2 werk.

U can bild yr collider in a playgrown,
bombard me wiv protons,
thro evrything u hav at me,
an 1 glorius day I will radee-ate 2 order.
I am de answer, earthlings,
now go figger out de kwestions.

Sulfur

She's a dazzler.
Some say, total drama queen.
It's true, if there's something to react to,
someone pushes her buttons,
she will react.

Left to her own devices, she's innocuous,
pottering around, pleasing herself
but watch for the warning signs,
changes of state,
that in-your-face yellow,
the dragon tattoo,
when she blows, she blows volcano
brimstone
the fires of hell
So don't, whatever you do,
get in her way.

Hydrogen

You can't hold me down for long,
buoyant, I'm ready to burn bright, pop.

Simple? Say straight forward,
there are no hidden layers to me.

Face value — that's what you get.
I say what I mean and I am what I am

a singular girl and
a star in the making.

If you think about it,
it's your all-natural pairing —

no need for a gooseberry neutron
my twin and I hold it together just fine.

Equations on Waking

You cling to the brink of sleep
Your eyelid flickers, mouth twitches
You move as
If it were dark as a shutdown mine
Dusky dizzy sweet; you breathe out
Your pulse beats
You teeter at the edge
Sunshine spoons around you. Closer
Your skin, we share
Skin's no barrier
Find   my
Quantum tunnelling through   you
In me.

In the thin light I watch your dream
I touch your night-rough chin
I kiss your jaw
I could still know your scent
I breathe
To my heart
I move, slow as dawn
My skin to
The warmth but
I analyse wave functions
Busy fundamental particles
And fragments of you

Lump

For now
it's just a lump
a like it or lump it
a one lump or two, a lump sum
the size of a two euro coin, a heads or tails
an is she or isn't she, all lumped in together
except it's only me, on my own, with my lump
and everywhere I go, my lump goes too

My thoughts circle it like a wary cat
like Schrödinger's cat neither dead nor alive
until someone opens the box

I have to hold it together for a few more days
I smile benignly, make believe I'm not terrified,
scared to touch it in case it's spread
so until my appointment
it's only a lump
right here.

She Stoops to Conker

Three sisters walked the towpath to gather
holly and cones for a winter display.
The locals tattled tales; I overheard —
Three sisters walked the towpath to gather
scarlet toadstools, moth wings, eye of blackbird —
a tastier tale this night than to say,
three sisters walked the towpath to gather
holly and cones for a winter display.

Conker

For Enda

Sometimes things happen along the way
while I sit on this wooden chair
waiting for my life to start.
A man comes along,
great, fine,
a child, another child,
wonderful, great
and this and that
and sometimes someone brings me a cup of tea
and sometimes someone brings me a letter
and once someone brought me a conker.

It sat on the palm of my hand
flawless gloss hard reflecting
the light bulb above my head,
caramel skin taut around its secret.
It sat on my palm.

It sits on my palm and the brightness goes
and I can't see the light in it.
It shrivels, wrinkles,
caves in on itself
and someone comes
and takes it away.

Monaghan Mosquitoes

There are mosquitoes in Monaghan the size of bats,
but easier to kill
and leave a tell-tale splat that swamps the bed.
But where there's one, there's more,
their whines as heavy as the dentist's drill.
They can suck the lifeblood out of a woman
in eight point two seconds flat.

At night, they crouch on my pillow
and chase me through my dreams,
drone homespun criticism —
All those words,
it's not very good, is it?
We've read it and it's rubbish;
there's no bite, nothing special.
We've read it all. Why do you bother?
Give it up, give it up.

That Broken Pot

The moon is new
and the heavy clouds are calm,
the wind has dropped,
yet still there is a tap-tapping
on your window.

Does it bother you?
That shiver, as if something's breath
has grazed, raised the hairs on your neck.
Why do you rise and draw the curtains
tight across the chink?

Peek out — the shadows steal towards you.
What is it startles next door's dog,
its barking, sudden to start, sudden to cease?
Not your cat,
she's hissing beneath your bed.

Who or what is watching? Believe what you will —
that crunch of gravel,
that scuffle at your sill
is not a fox nor swooping owl.
Did you lock the back door? Are you sure?

The crows are roosting in high branches;
it is not they who claw through your bins
for numbers, dates, addresses,
leaving scattered shreds,
breaking that pot you find in the morning.

Unintentional Installation
For Tríona

So little depends upon
a broken wheelbarrow
its jammed wheel awkward
in the gallery lawn
mud rusted to the struts.

Was the barrow once red?
No one cares
to remember:
What matter?

Soft rain falls
worms rise and soon
chickens will emerge
in a burst
of white noise.

Grange Castle Haiku

I am late for work —
I park amid the stragglers
halfway to Finglas

Phelim wants Mark's job
Mark's more than a match for Niamh
Niamh's soft on Phelim

Cathal winks at me
chats up the girls in QA
we'll do all he asks

Sunshine at lunchtime
we slip from shadowed buildings
winter pale faces

Health and Safety bleat —
walk don't run, hold the hand rail
don't fall and sue us

Maria comes in —
we stop googling cheap breaks
change screens to spreadsheets

Here are no seasons —
we wear the same clothes year round,
watch weather through glass

What a wasted day —
the afternoon spent fixing
the broken morning

Evening's clock hand crawls
minute to dawdled minute
time treacles to five

The sun shines all day —
clouds roll in from Dublin Bay
by five it's raining

Hi-tech glass building
as I leave, I pinch myself —
this is where I work

Karl
after Tim Minchin

An overpriced restaurant, you know the sort,
sludge-coloured velvet, uncomfortable chairs.
It's a big work do for some bigwig tiger
and I'm on a warning for my best behaviour,
rigged out and tagging along
with Himself, the tiger cub and me, the WAG.

The table's set with square plates and round glasses.
We mingle with some work blokes
with notions of promotions, some single,
some with wives in tight dresses and tight lips.

At the centre the honoured guest,
barrel-chest bursting out of his best pink shirt,
holding forth on Asian economies, trading currencies
taxation strategies including
'a double Irish with a Dutch sandwich,'
which is not something to eat.

My stomach growls as he grips my hand,
eyes gliding down my chest,
checks my ass, determines me to be
of no import, no threat.

Karl's his name, After Marx? I say,
triggering a laugh that jiggles his belly
and a slap on the back that would floor a yak.
Himself does that 'be good' look at me.
And I try.

But Karl's not trying. He slurps oysters and ticks boxes.
Merc. Tick. Race Horse. Tick. Rolex. Tick tock.
Second wife, blonde, tick, with admirable assets. Tick tock.
I rearrange mine and tighten my lips.

We weave around conversational sinkholes, as he ploughs
into his half-a-bloody-cow, chewing open-mouthed
as if we all want to savour the flavour,
his nose now as rosy as the bloody good Bordeaux
he sloshes in our glasses.

They've moved on to golf and he goes out on the course
every week, walking the talk,
addressing the ball and pressing the flesh.
It's all about who you know, he says.
Scratch my back and maybe, who knows. Do you scratch?

My back is itching now.
I'd rather, I say, watch wood warp than whack a ball
up a field to a tiny, tiny hole.
He repeats that backslap and I cough up
some pasta across the table at Himself
who does that look again and changes tack
back to stock on the rise and the price of houses.

Karl has cash in Buda and Pest.
Property's through the roof
and the roof isn't on yet but he's sitting pretty
waiting to flip them on some poor hick
who actually wants to live there.

The talk's of percentage leverage
and the bankers hurling cash at him
and the Euribor and bore is what he is.
My cheeks are aching with not yawning but I bury
my grievances in more Berry Pavlova
and when he shoulders outside for a smoke,
I gripe to Himself, ignore his chides
which slide off me like ice cream on a very hot tart.

Karl sweeps back yapping on a phone as cool as the night.
Have to keep Herself happy, he says
and click-clacks the apps to zoom in on his flats
on Google maps and track his stock
on the Iseq and the Nasdaq and the bond rates
and all manner of things I don't want or need.

It's time to shed all the deadwood, he says, ship them back
to Brazzaville and Riga. I confess I have to google
Brazzaville later (It's The Congo).
But he's all for diversity as long as the service industry
speaks English with no accent.

Before I can stop myself, I say, Like no one from Tralee?
Or Bristol or Dundee?
That's different, he says. My wife's from Surrey.
Not her fault, I say. How about Cape Town
or Sydney? Quebec? Tennessee?
That's fine.
So where's the line? Hong Kong, Nairobi?
Singapore or Delhi?
I'm on a roll here and he's all bluster.
I exert all the self-control I can muster
and shut up.

But not for long. He keeps on.
It's the New Celtic economy.
Speculate to accumulate. And if those cadgers and shirkers
and pram-faced mothers got off their arses and got jobs.
Give me your tired, your poor, I start.
Yeah, your huddled masses will bring this country to its knees.
Living off the state like it's a right? Off taxpayers
like you and me, the producers,
the shafters, the movers and grafters.

And don't get me started on state-subsidised art.
Get a real fucking job, he says.

Himself is rolling his eyes like a big black bull
but I'm all riled up now, to my chagrin surprised
that people like Karl actually exist
and think anyone else would believe
such bollocks. Yeah, don't get me started, he says.
And I don't.

'Cos Himself has moved on to the pleading look,
more effective than bulls' eyes.
'Cos what's the point? Karl's a prick,
he won't listen to me, take anything I say on board.
Wrong job, wrong school, wrong team, wrong town,
no big swinging dick.

So I take immense, hot-air-balloon pleasure
when I see Karl's big blustered face now in the news,
day after day, self-justifying, pontificating
on the New New Celtic economy,
denying the assets that he threw
with admirable timing and admirable haste
on his still admirably assetted, but now ex-wife
was nothing more than a fluke.

She's moved on now, the ex-wife, took the children,
changed the locks, sold the wine cellar
and golf clubs on eBay, so they say.
And actually, take a look around, Karl,
there's no one left now admiring you at all.

Flaming for Vincent

Oh give me a red-headed man
with fisherman hands that can gut a salmon
or mend a dry stone wall
and in the next moment, pick an eyelash from my cheek
to paint the suggestion of cracks on canvas.

Oh give me a red-headed man
with a thick matching beard
to roughen my skin with kisses.
I'll wallow in the man-scent of his collar,
probe the hollow at his throat with my tongue tip.

Oh give me a red-headed man
with flecked, forget-me-not eyes.
I'll smother his freckled back in factor 50,
love him something rotten
on the green tartan blanket.

Oh give me a red-headed man
with lumberjack thighs.
He'll show me off to his soot-headed buddies,
cycle home before closing
and take his time with me.

Oh give me a red-headed man
with fire in his heart.
I'll fill his belly with porter cake,
make jam from the hedgerows,
honey-roast the parsnips he digs from the garden.

Oh give me a red-headed man
and I'll give him a barrow-load of red-headed bairns
with candyfloss cheeks and milkshake smiles.

We'll picnic on the green tartan blanket;
I'll mother their tender, freckled skin in factor 50.

O Lord, please, I'm burning up
for a red-headed man.

Lying in our Morning Bed

Hip bone by hip bone, I describe for you
the just-born gazelle or whatever it was,
more legs than body
more hoof than brain, for certain sure,
suckling from a leopardess.

What acquaintance had this lone fawn
with the dangers of this world
save the blood of its own birth —
that slither to the earth?
Why not get it over with straight off?
Life can be too full of loss.

You shift beside me.
No it was fine, nothing happened.
I spread my arms, my neck exposed.
Don't get up.

Slow Poison 1944

That winter, the snows came early.
The small ones forgot,
but I dreamt of oven-fresh bread.

The soldiers stole our cow, our pig,
left three hens hidden in the barn.
We took them one by one.

Carrots and apples, potatoes and beans,
wheat and oatcakes, turnips and beets.
There were always people knocking.

We trapped vermin.
The cats disappeared, first the ginger
then the rest. The dogs ran in packs.

They sent Pa to the factories.
Ma burned the big wardrobe
and grew fragile as twigs.

We ground acorns, boiled nettles, dandelions,
dug up her bulbs, tulip and iris,
gouged out their little yellow hearts.

Hubie is Wearing his Uniform

It hangs from his bony shoulders, pressed, starched
so stiff it would stay upright if he fell

The hollows on his face trace history,
his medals glint, his cap at regulation angle

Above this country fair, dark against the summer sky
first black then red blue green chutes float

down, helix over the sun-squinting crowd
falling like ashes from a fire

They become men, then soldiers fresh returned
skulls clean shaven, chests barrelled

Closer, closer, they land one by one,
big boots precise on the cloth cross

Deft, they scoop the silks and stow them
Turning, their faces are older than their rank

They line up, march straight and smart
to where Hubie waits, snap a salute

He unbends to attention, returns it,
hand shaky to his temple. Applause.

But behind creep shadows, lists
of names and places, ages, dates,

photos, posed and proud, so young
and others, the unpictured, unnamed,

maimed on dusty roads, careless hardware
drones flown far on flickering screens

clouds of thistledown
drifting through the fair.

We Keep our Old Defences

We keep our old defences,
first the wave-worn Watchers,
sturdy Sleepers, the second line
then Dreamers around our land.

Our dykes protect us. See from the top,
over there the sea and down there the low polders.
Diagonal rails and drainage ditches
keep the sleepy waters sluiced and channelled,
hold our placid stock in their place.
See the neat boxes, how dense our market gardens grow,
that's the work of generations, centuries of control.

We've no room here for any more.
Breaching our borders would be chaos,
all that we've made for ourselves
— flooded, overwhelmed, transformed.

Imagine if we let them crumble,
welcomed the migrations surging in,
a new high tide washing all before it,
as in slow succession
the Watchers,
then Sleepers,
then Dreamers
give way.

Watchers, Sleepers and Dreamers are the three levels of sea defences in Holland.

Verbatim

i.m Barbara Ennis Price

It's all the fault of the British, she said.
The cursing came in with the troopers,
the other ranks and their wives as bad.
Before that, we Irish never swore.
No curse would pass our tender lips,
no drop of whiskey,
no beatings, no casual cruelty.
Sure, weren't we a gentle race
until the squaddies boated in?
We were milk and honey,
the soft heads of babes, the pigs at Christmas,
root vegetables and stone walls.
What did we have to swear about
until the British came?

An Agreeable Afternoon
For Maeve

Two ladies elegantly dressed,
  Yes
clip-on pearls and hair fresh set
pink lipstick spiders up wrinkles
widows' rings loose to the knuckles,
  Yes
slip on their wide fit shoes
take up their metal walking sticks
and meet in the hotel café,
  Yes
to split a slice of Cherry Bakewell
too hefty for one
two forks please,
  Yes
and in a nod to modern times
two lattes in glasses
with chocolate sprinkles,
  Yes

Did I tell you
Do you remember
Would you say she
Have you heard that
  Yes

to spend a pleasant afternoon,
  Yes!
agreeing with each other.

She was the Queen of the Butterfly Bun

Snowed with icing sugar drifts
the top sliced, wings
balanced on sweet cream
perfection on a china plate

Peel the papercase away
the ridges, soft and crumbled
release the calm vanilla
its subtle power scents remembrance

Breathe in, your nostrils flare
hold back, not yet, not yet
moisten your lips, saliva flows
now, open your mouth, bite

Is it as good as hers were?
Pillow soft and light as daisies
let your tongue take the fullness of it
swallow, probe out the final crumb.

Email, Three Poems Attached

Professor, may I call you Brendan?
We met last week after you read,
not long enough to tune in to each other's ways.
Do you recall?

          As we descended, step by step,
I told my tale of the wheelchair man tipping over the pavement lip,
me poised arms open; he hadn't slipped,
thank the lord, neither of us would have liked that;
he was an elephant of a man.

Half a glass of red wine, Brendan and the words come tumbling out.
I can witter on until the black Kerry cows
wander up Parnell Street to meet us.
I'll say anything.

          Remember me now, Brendan?
I don't know what you heard but at the bottom of the stairs
you hugged me and said I'd been looking for it.
What did you think I was offering, Brendan?
Only a croggie on my Dublin Bike.

If you're game, you can still hop on and we'll freewheel
past the Rotunda, the Gate, down O'Connell Street,
me on the pedals, you on the saddle,
our coats flapping together like two blackbirds,
my orange scarf slipstream,
your hand holding your cap, the other on my waist.

We'll cruise by the Gresham, the GPO,
salute Jim Larkin, Penneys and Eason's,
puff through the lights, fly over the Liffey and I'll have you back in Trinity
before you can compose a couplet, poetry to my arse.

Maybe, Brendan, if that new blue carpet had upset you
and you had stumbled into my arms,
if I were ten years younger or twenty, things would be different.
But you'd have taken the stairs two at a time and I'd have said nothing,
had nothing to say.

This could be the beginning.
Would you read my poems, Brendan?
Would you take me under your wing?

By Strawberry Beds

Morning drives golden through Strawberry Beds,
pale sun skims the horizon, pinks the clouds,
frosts each leaf in a glittering sheath.
Here the real Liffey runs
not yet retarded to slime-walled, urban grey.
River mist rises like ghostly dancers.

Blue Toyota Woman pouts in the mirror,
slicks on coral lipstick, smoothes her eyebrow
with a licked fingertip, fluffs her hair.
Dirty Jeep Man cricks his phone to his neck
arms flapping affirmation.
We edge under the M50 bridge.

On the radio, AA Roadwatch says,
it's bumper to bumper from Blanchardstown.
Above the traffic flows.
Chapelizod ponies drink, heads shaggy to the water,
they examine their reflections,
flicking their manes like schoolgirls.

Shifting down gears to the Phoenix Park,
deer nose the shaded grasses,
antlers blasé like living sculptures.
A helmeted cyclist freewheels towards the church.
The President's home. I wave,
he doesn't wave back.

Cresting the next hill, Dublin spreads before me
a frozen stage of spires, towers and crane upon crane
stretching gracefully out of the grey.
Out and round past the Guinness stacks,
Emmanuel from Nigeria hands out *The Metro*,
his grin infectious, wide and white.

I pull into Heuston with plenty of time
and there's a message from you on my phone.
I pause to text.
It's a beautiful morning in Dublin.

Essence

Do you get that smell? Sweet sour hops drift upwind,
mists ripple the Liffey, ghost the quays,
ruffle three buskers on O'Connell Street.
Beshoff's chip papers batter takeaway lattes.

There's fresh oranges on Mary Street,
fresh words, fresh sprayed on concrete walls.
Port containers sigh out in a diesel cloud;
sea-salty air sloshes a swill of spills in gutters.

The brutal stink of bins in puddled alleys
mingles with stale heat stealing from pub doors,
the flare of matches, a cigarette catches
and someone somewhere soothes a honey saxophone.

Pure Class

The wide bit at the top's the colour of Dublin Bus —
Number 13, upstairs.
Then a stripe of Rory's bike, the flash one that got robbed,
and there's my school tie, manky looking yellow.
Then comes the orange in the tricolour, flying over Grange Castle.
That one's like when Siobhán went mad on fake tan.
That bit's Gran's flesh-coloured knickers, hanging on the line.
Below that's the Lucozade they used buy me down Polly Hops pub.
The pink there near the bottom's my auntie's lipstick,
she's gonna get me one the same for my birthday.
And scarlet's the colour my cheeks would go
if they knew I was writing poems again.
Poetry won't get you outta here, my da says.

All them colours together in the one sky,
it makes you think though.
Class that sky is, pure class.

Only Six Minutes of Normal Time Remain

Only six minutes of normal time remain
then it gets weird
the fouled forward dives into the grass
with a splash
and is never seen again

The backs run the centre half
into four fifths forward and offside
off bottom, off top,
off the other side of underneath,
outside, through side and far side.

The keeper calls handball and eyeball
crystal ball, hairball,
basket ball and basket case.

There's a free kick,
a paid kick, a cheap kick,
cheap trick, cheap skate,
but he makes the save
save face, save as you earn
save my soul to the corner.

It hits the goalposts,
moves the goalposts, posts the move-goal,
posts the red card,
the purple card, the green card to America

and he's sent off
sent away, off the scent
and on the bench,
on the rocker, off his rocker

watching the linesman
the circlesman, the small parallelogram
till the whistle blows, wets
and stops.

A City with Stones of Gold

I knew a city with golden stones,
a place of scholars. We the chosen
shucked the limits of our hometown grime
and plundered there — a precious time.

We crammed it in; I think we knew
but didn't know how rare it was, grew
like spires, bathed hot in the glow
danced bright together as the hue

stripped the provinces from our flesh,
gilded us one by one with leaf
thin as whispers, bonded us
and wrote a lifetime of dreams.

The walls buttressed us until
we thought ourselves capable of standing,
unsupported, some fell
tarnished, some never stood at all,

some flew.

Tell Me about your Scar

that pucker of skin in the shape of an owl.
Was it an irritable pug,
a fight about a man, a look, the price of pie?
Were you cursed by Minerva?
Did your knife slip making a rocket from a bottle?

Is it perhaps where you had a rash tattoo removed?
I hear the laser hurts more than the needle.
Were you caught climbing barbed wire into somewhere,
out of somewhere?
Did you fly into a window, smash a mirror?

Was it cancer, may I ask, a nasty melanoma?
Did a small owl-shaped alien erupt after one too many bad nights?
Was it self-inflicted?
Is there a matching half on your other arm,
your leg, your brother?

Does it ache when storms are near?
Do you still notice it?
Does it disappear in sunshine,
in the shower, in the snow,
when you sweat, when you fall in love?

Do you have a story
or shall I make you one?
I can do that.
Sit still,
this will hardly hurt a bit.

What to do with my Ashes

When I die, cremate me.
Drop me in a bucket
of soapy water and mix well
with a wooden spoon.

Incant, if you feel the urge, sing songs,
read poems, tell stories, don't cry.
Then take some metal coat-hangers
and twist a circle, one each.

Go to a wide open space, you choose —
somewhere nice you can revisit —
dunk your loops in the suds
and take turns to blow big, beautiful bubbles.

Release me over the river, into the trees,
up to the wide blue sky and say goodbye,
as with each glistening globe
I float away.

Mash

I was at a village fete
with you in the sunshine,
hand in hand
bouncy castle, tombola, homemade jam.

I judged the mashed potato contest
giving marks for presentation, flavour, consistency.
The winner, a dimpled woman of Amish appearance.
What's your secret? I asked before I woke.
It's about love, she said, all about love.

ACKNOWLEDGEMENTS

Acknowlegements are due to the following publications in which versions of some of these poems were published: *Abridged; Authors and Artists Introductions* (Windows Publications); *The Backyards of Heaven; Anthology of Contemporary Poetry from Ireland and Newfoundland & Labrador; Boyne Berries; The Carlin's Kist; Crannog; 'Day and Night' South Dublin CC/New Island; The Great Book of Maynooth; The Grist Anthology of New Writing; The Longford Leader; Magma* (UK); *The Moth; New Leaf* (Germany); *North West Words; Obsessed with Pipework* (UK); *Orbis* (UK); *Pickled Body; Poetry Bus; Poetry Ireland Review; Red Lamp Black Piano: The Cáca Milis Cabaret Anthology; Revival; Ropes; Science Meets Poetry 3: ESOF2012; Skylight 47; The SHOp; Southlight* (UK); *Stinging Fly; Stony Thursday; The Sunday Tribune;* and the *Tallaght Echo.*

Some Poems, a chapbook containing several of the poems published in this collection, was published by The Moth Editions in 2011.

'Thorium 238' was exhibited at the Radcliffe Science Library, Oxford; 'She Stoops to Conker' was exhibited on the Rochdale Canal; 'Let's Go Driving' was exhibited at the Peace Camp Poems at the Poetry Café, London; 'Amsterdam Otto Recommends' was displayed on a lamppost as part of Upstart Art.

I am grateful for bursaries from the Arts Council, Kildare County Council Arts Service and South Dublin County Council Arts Office and a writing residency at the Oberpfälzer Künstlerhaus in Germany from the Tyrone Guthrie Centre which allowed me valuable time to write. Thanks are also due first to my family, Denis, Joe and Grace; to the Maynooth Writers' group and the Atrium Writers who workshopped many poems; Dermot Bolger who encouraged me early on; Will Govan and Rebecca O'Connor at The Moth; John Walsh and Lisa Frank at Doire Press; and the fabulous Poetry Divas, Maeve O'Sullivan, Barbara Smith and Tríona Walsh, along with many other fellow writers who have inspired and supported me.

KATE DEMPSEY is from Coventry and studied Physics at Oxford University. She lived and worked in the UK; Nijmegen, The Netherlands and Albuquerque, New Mexico before settling in Ireland. She has lived in Maynooth, County Kildare with her family for more than twenty years. Prizes for her writing include The Plough Prize, Cecil Day Lewis Award, shortlisting for the Hennessy New Irish Writing Award for both Poetry and Fiction and two commendations for the Patrick Kavanagh Award. She was nominated for the Forward Prize and selected to read for Poetry Ireland Introductions. She runs the Poetry Divas, a collective of women poets who blur the wobbly boundary between page and stage at events and festivals all over Ireland.